100% alpaca

Artesano yarns are made from the best quality natural fibres. This range of 14 exclusive patterns has been designed by the world renowned Jean Moss.

The patterns are designed for use with Artesano Hummingbird alpaca DK or Artesano standard DK 100% pure alpaca.

For more information regarding our yarns and our patterns, you can call us on +44(0)118 9503350 or visit our website www.artesanoyarns.co.uk

Please note that due to printing processes, colours will appear slightly different to the actual yarns. Yarn weights are approximate as all knitters may produce slightly different tensions. It is recommended to knit a tension square prior to a project. Text and patterns copyright Jean Moss 2007 Copyright in the work, Artesano Ltd. First Published in the UK in 2007 by Artesano Ltd.©

ABBREVIATIONS

cm(s)	centimetre(s)	ev	every
in(s)	inch(es)	beg	beginning
m	metres	rem	remaining
g	grams	k2tog	knit 2 sts together
oz	ounces	p2tog	purl 2 sts together
yd(s)	yard(s)	k3tog	knit 3 sts together
mm	millimetres	p3tog	purl 3 sts together
st(s)	stitch(es)	tbl	through back loop
dpn(s)	double pointed needle(s)	sl	slip
WS	right-side	psso	pass slipped st over
RS	wrong-side	ssk	(slip, slip, knit) – slip next 2 sts knitwise, one at a time to RH needle. Insert tip of LH needle into fronts of these sts from left to right and knit them together
k	knit		
p	purl		
st st	stocking stitch		
no	number		
rep	repeat		
ndle(s)	needle(s)		
cont	continue		
foll	following/follows	slip 2-k1-p2sso	slip 2 sts purlwise, k1, then pass 2 slipped sts over
c.o.e	cast on edge		
alt	alternate		
dec	decrease	yo	yarn over needle to make 1 st
inc	increase		
patt	pattern	yf	yarn to front of work
		yb	yarn to back of work

CHULO

GRAFFITI

DECO

CHILL

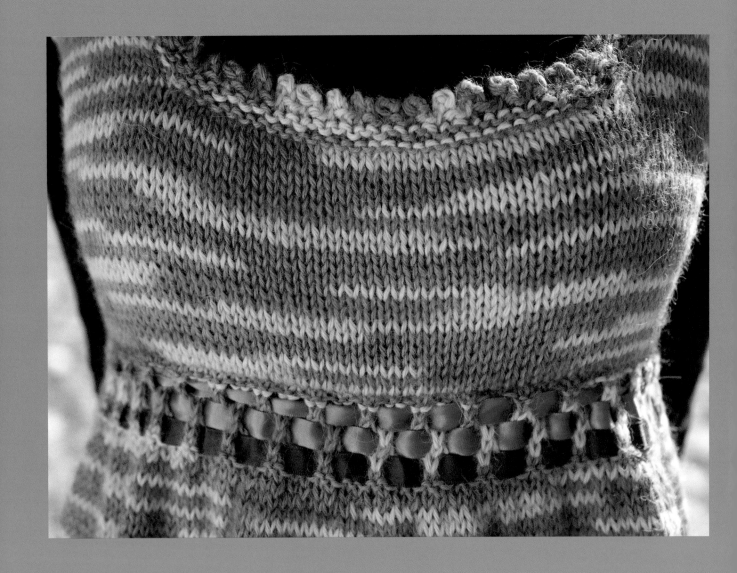

BOP

RAPT

CHRYSALIS

TWISTER

JAZZ

SNUG

HUG

LACED

BOO

STORM

CHULO

SIZES
S, M & L - finished size 18(20, 22)" [46(51, 56) cm] circumference. Figures in parenthesis relate to S, M, L and XL sizes respectively. When there is only one figure, this relates to all.

YARN
ARTESANO Hummingbird: (327yds/300m per 150g hank):1 hank WOODPECKER
NB Yarn is used double throughout

NEEDLES
One pair 5 mm (US 8)
One pair 6 mm (US 10) or size to obtain tension. We recommend Brittany needles

TENSION
16 sts and 20 rows = 4"/10 cms over st st. Please work swatch and check carefully. If wrong alter size of needles until correct tension is achieved.

STITCHES
Garter Stitch
Knit every stitch
Stocking Stitch

RS rows   Knit
WS rows   Purl

TO MAKE HAT
Ear Flaps- Make 2.
Using smaller needles, cast on 5 sts and knit 4 rows. Change to larger needles and cont in st st to end as foll:
Row 1(RS)   k2, m2 (knit into front, back and front again of next st), k2 – 7 sts
Row 2   p2, k3, p2
Row 3   k2, m1 (knit into front and back of next st), k1, m1, k2 – 9 sts
Row 4   p2, k5, p2
Row 5   k2, m1, k3, m1, k2 – 11 sts
Row 6   p2, k7, p2
Row 7   k2, m1, k5, m1, k2 – 13 sts
Row 8   p2, k9, p2
Row 9   k2, m1, k7, m1, k2 – 15 sts
Row 10   p2, k11, p2
Row 11   k2, m1, k9, m1, k2 – 17 sts
Row 12   p2, k13, p2
Row 13   knit
Row 14   p2, k13, p2
M & L
Rows 15-18 Repeat rows 13 and 14 twice.
S
Rows 15-16 Repeat rows 13 and 14 once.
Break yarn and leave sts on holder.

HAT
Using smaller needles, cast on 10(12, 14) sts. then with RS facing knit 17 sts from holder, cast on a further 20(23, 27) sts, then with RS facing knit 17 sts from other holder, cast on a further 10(12, 14) sts – 74(81, 89) sts. Work in garter st for 5 rows. Change to larger needles and cont in st st to end, starting on RS row.
When work measures 6(6, 6.5)" [15.25(15.25,16.5) cm] from cast-on edge, ending on
WS row, **shape crown:**
Row 1   * k4, k2tog; repeat from * to last 2(3, 5) sts k2(3,5) - 62(68, 75) sts
Row 2   purl
Row 3   * k3, k2tog; repeat from * to last 2(3, 0) sts k2(3, 0)- 50(55, 60) sts
Row 4   purl
Row 5   * k2, k2tog; repeat from * to last 2(3, 0) sts k2(3, 0) - 38(42, 45) sts
Row 6   purl
Row 7   * k1, k2tog; repeat from * to last 2(0, 0) sts, k2(0, 0) - 26(28, 30) sts
Row 8   purl
Row 9   *k2tog across row - 13(14, 15) sts
Row 10   purl
Row 11   *k2tog across row – 7(7, 8) sts
Row 12   purl
Break off yarn, thread through remaining sts and secure firmly on inside.

FINISHING
Oversew back seam on inside.
Plaited cords-Make 2

PLAITED CORDS

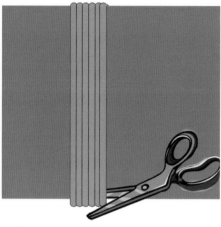

Wind yarn around card as in diagram, six times and cut along bottom edge

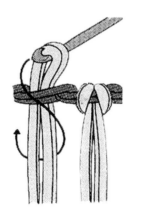

Attach to bottom edge of one earflap (as in diagram), then using four strands together, plait the yarn until it measures 10" (25.5cm). Knot the cord, leaving a tassle of approx 1.25" (3cm)

GRAFFITI

SIZES
XS (to fit bust 32"/81cm)
S (to fit bust 34"/86cm)
M (to fit bust 36"/91cm)
L (to fit bust 38"/96cm)
XL (to fit bust 40"/101cm)
- see schematic for actual measurements.
Figures in parenthesis relate to S, M, L and XL sizes respectively. When there is only one figure, this relates to all.

YARN
ARTESANO Hummingbird:
(327yds/300m per 150g hank):
4(4, 4, 5, 5) hanks LAPWING

NEEDLES
3.25 mm (US 3) and 4 mm (US 6);
or size to obtain tension stitch holders; large crochet hook. We recommend Brittany Needles

NOTIONS
2 zippers – open-ended 20.5(20.5, 21, 21.5, 21,5)")" [52(52, 53.5, 54.5, 54.5)cm] for centre front,

the other 9(9, 9.5, 10, 10.5)" [22.75(23, 24, 25.5, 26.5)cm]to fit top of hood.

TENSION
22 sts and 28 rows = 4"/10 cms over st st. Please work swatch and check carefully. If wrong alter size of needles until correct tension is achieved.

STITCHES
Garter Stitch
Knit every row
Stocking Stitch
Knit on RS rows and purl on WS rows

BACK
Using smaller straight needles, cast on 90(96, 102, 108, 114) sts. Work 6 rows in garter st, then change to larger needles and cont in st st to end. When work measures 2" [5cm] from cast on edge ending on WS row, dec as foll:
XS, S & M 1 st at both ends of next,then ev foll 6th row 7(7, 7,) times – 74(80, 86) sts
L & XL 1 st at both ends of next, then ev foll 7th row 7(7) times - 92(98) sts.
Cont in st st as set for 11(11, 11, 10, 10) rows, then inc as foll:
XS, S & M 1 st at both ends of next, then ev foll 5th row 7 times – 90(96, 102) sts

L & XL 1 st at both ends of next, then ev foll 4th row 7 times – 108(114) sts

Cont as set until work measures 15.5" [39.5 cm] from cast on edge ending on a WS row, then **shape armhole:** Cast off 4(5, 5, 6, 6) sts at beg of next 2 rows. Dec 1 st at both ends of next and ev foll alt row 5(6, 8, 9, 11) times in all – 72(74, 76, 78, 80)sts. Cont until work measures 22.25(22.25, 22.75, 23.25, 23.25)" [56.5(56.5, 57.75, 59, 59)cm] from cast on edge ending on WS row, then **shape shoulder and neck:** Next row (RS) Work 22sts, place centre 28(30, 32, 34, 36) sts on holder, join a second ball of yarn and work to end. **Working both sides at the same time,** dec 1 st at both neck edges on next and foll alt row.

At the same time work and place 6 sts on holder at armhole edge on next row, (for left back neck it will be foll row), and 7 sts on foll **alt** row. Cast off over all 20sts.

LEFT FRONT
Using smaller straight needles, cast on 45(48, 51, 54, 57) sts. Work 6 rows in garter st, then change to larger needles and cont as foll to end:

Next row knit
Next row k3, purl to end
Cont in this way in st st, keeping the 3 sts of garter st at centre front to end.
When work measures 2" [5cm] from cast on edge ending on WS row, dec as foll:
XS, S & M 1 st at beg of next, then ev foll 6th row 7(7, 7,) times – 37(40, 43) sts
L & XL 1 st at beg of next, then at armhole edge on ev foll 7th row 7(7) times - 46(49) sts.
Cont in st st as set for 11(11, 11, 10, 10) rows, then inc as foll:
XS, S & M 1 st at beg of next, then at armhole edge on ev foll 5th row 7 times – 45(48, 51) sts
L & XL 1 st at beg of next, then ev foll 4th row 7 times – 54(57) sts
At the same time when work measures 3" [7.5cm] from cast on edge ending on WS row, **work pocket:** Work and place on holder 10(11, 11, 12, 12) sts. Re-join yarn to rem sts and dec 1 st at beg of 1st row, then at pocket edge every 5 rows 7 times. Leave sts on holder.
Return to 10(11, 11, 12, 12) sts on holder, rejoin yarn and cast on 26(26,26,28, 30)sts. Keeping shaping correct at outside edge, work

35 rows in st st, casting off 18(18, 18, 20, 22) sts at beg of final row. Work across all 37(40, 43, 46, 49) sts and cont with shaping as above.
Cont as set until work measures 15.5" [39.5 cm] from cast on edge ending on a WS row, then **shape armhole:** Cast off 4(5, 5, 6, 6) sts at beg of next row. Work 1 row, then dec 1 st at beg of next and ev foll alt row 5(6, 8, 9, 11) times in all.
Cont until work measures 20.5(20.5, 21, 21.5, 21,5)")" [52(52, 53.5, 54.5, 54.5)cm] from cast on edge ending on RS row, then **shape neck:** Work and place 10(11, 12, 13, 14) sts on holder, then dec 1 st at beg of next and ev foll alt row 6 times in all – 20 sts.
Cont until work measures 22.25(22.25, 22.75, 23.25, 23.25)" [56.5(56.5, 57.75, 59, 59)cm] from cast on edge ending on WS row, then **work shoulder:** Work and place 6 sts on holder at armhole edge on next row, and 7 sts on foll **alt** row. Cast off over all 20 sts.

RIGHT FRONT
Work as for left front reversing all shapings and pockets and centre front band.

SLEEVES
Using smaller needles, cast on 50(50, 54, 58, 58) sts.

Work 6 rows in garter stitch, then change to larger needles and cont in st st to end, inc as foll:

XS 1 st at both ends of 21st, then ev foll 22nd row 4 times– 60 sts.

S 1 st at both ends of 15th, then ev foll 16th row 6 times – 64 sts

M 1 st at both ends of 15th, then ev foll 16th row 6 times – 68 sts

L 1 st at both ends of 15th, then ev foll 14th row 7 times – 74 sts

XL 1 st at both ends of 15th, then ev foll 10th row 9 times – 78 sts

Cont until work measures 18(18, 18.25, 18.5, 18.5)" [45.75(45.75, 46.5, 47, 47)cm] from cast on edge ending on WS row and then **shape sleeve cap:**

Cast off 4(5, 5, 6, 6) sts at beg of next 2 rows. Then dec 1 st at both ends of ev 3rd row 2(2, 4, 2, 0) times, then ev alt row 13(13, 11, 15, 18) times – 22(24, 28, 28, 30)sts.

Cast off 2 sts at beg of next 4 rows,. Cast off rem 14(16, 20, 20, 22) sts

FINISHING

Use a small neat backstitch on edge of work for all seams except welts, where an invisible slip stitch should be used. Join shoulder seams.

Hood

Using smaller needles, with right side facing and starting at right centre front, pick up and k10(11, 12, 13, 14) sts from holder at centre front, k12 sts up sloping edge of neck, k6 sts up straight side of neck, k2 sts down back neck, k28(30, 32, 34, 36) sts from holder at centre back, k2 sts up other side back neck, k6 sts down left front neck edge, k12 sts down sloping edge of neck and k10(11, 12, 13, 14) sts from holder at left centre front – 88(92, 96, 100, 104) sts. Working in garter stitch, cont until work measures 13" [33 cm] and then cast off.

Pocket edgings

Using smaller needles, with right side facing, pick up and k 34 sts along sloping edge of pockets. Knit 5 rows and then cast off knitwise. Slip stitch side edges at top and bottom to sweater. Sew pocket linings in place on inside using invisible slip stitch.

Insert sleeves placing any fullness evenly over top of sleeve cap. Join side and sleeve seams in one line, leaving thumb-size gap 1" [2.5 cm] from cuff edge. Sew open-ended zips into front and along top edge of hood, zipper to be at centre back of hood when closed. Position the zip two stitches in from the edge to prevent the teeth from showing and sew in place with a backstitch.

Tassle

Measure out 10 x 18" [45 cm] pieces of yarn. Fold in two and thread folded end through zipper fastener. Attach the tassel by pulling the threads through the loop formed. Trim to preferred length.

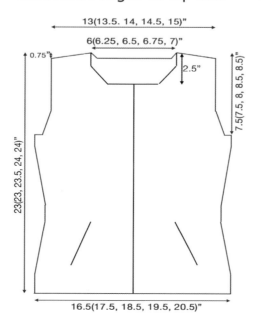

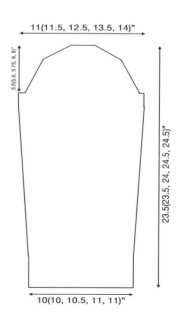

DECO

SIZES

One size 9" [23 cm] long and 12.5 [31.75 cm] wide - see schematic

YARN

ARTESANO Hummingbird: (327yds/300m per 150g hank):1 hank MALLARD (used double)

NEEDLES

4 mm (US 6) and 5 mm (US 8); or size to obtain tension cable needle, stitch markers We recomend using Brittany birchwood needles.

NOTIONS

6" [15 cm] diameter circular cane handles

TENSION

16 sts and 26 rows = 4"/10 cms over moss st. Please work swatch and check carefully. If wrong alter size of needles until correct tension is achieved.

STITCHES

Moss (or Seed) Stitch
Row 1   *k1, p1; repeat from * to end
Row 2   Knit the purl sts and purl the knit stitches
Repeat row 2
Stocking Stitch
RS rows   Knit
WS rows   Purl
1 x 1 Rib
*k1, p1, rep across 1st row; on subsequent rows keep knit and purl sts correct.

ABBREVIATIONS

C3f   Slip 3 stitches onto cable needle (cn) and hold at front of work, k3, k3 from cn
C3b   Slip 3 stitches onto cn and hold at back of work, k3, k3 from cn

BACK & FRONT

(both alike)
NB Use two strands of yarn. Using larger needles cast on 61 sts and work as foll:
Row 1 (RS)p2, k12, (p1, k1) 16 times, p1, k12, p2
Row 2   k2, p12, (p1, k1) 16 times, p13, k2
Row 3   p2, k12, k2tog, (p1, k1) 14 times, p1, k2tog, k12, p2
Row 4   k2, p12, (k1, p1) 15 times, k1, p12, k2
Row 5   p2, c3f, c3b, (k1, p1) 15 times, k1, c3f, c3b, p2
Row 6   k2, p12, (k1, p1) 15 times, k1, p12, k2
Row 7   p2, k12, p2tog, (k1, p1) 13 times, k1, p2tog, k12, p2
Row 8   k2, p12, (p1, k1) 14 times, p13, k2
Row 9   p2, k12, (p1, k1) 14 times, p1, k12, p2
Row 10   k2, p12, (p1, k1) 14 times, p13, k2
Row 11   p2, k12, k2tog, (p1, k1) 12 times, p1, k2tog, k12, p2
Row 12   k2, p12, (k1, p1) 13 times, k1, p12, k2
Row 13   p2, k12, (k1, p1) 13 times, k13, p2
Row 14   k2, p12, (k1, p1) 13 times, k1, p12, k2
Row 15   p2, c3f, c3b, p2tog, (k1, p1) 11 times, k1, p2tog, c3f, c3b, p2
Row 16   k2, p12, (p1, k1) 12 times, p13, k2
Cont in patt as set above decreasing 1 st at both ends (inside cables) every 4th row until there are 31 sts (59 rows) and cabling every 10th row (rows 5, 15, 25, 35, 45, 55), keeping moss st correct in between.

Next row (WS) Knit (for fold line). Then change to smaller needles and work a further 1" [2.5 cm] in 1 x 1 rib, increasing 1 st at both ends of 3rd and 7th rows. Cast off on larger needles.

FINISHING

With right sides facing and using a small backstitch on very edge of work, stitch together front and back of bag along three sides, starting and finishing 2" [5 cm] from top edge, leaving cast off edge open. Then using smaller needles, with RS facing and starting where rib begins, pick up and knit 10 sts down open top edge of bag and 10 sts up other side. Cast off. Slipstitch ribs in place on inside, after inserting one handle in each before stitching. If preferred line with silk.

SCHEMATIC

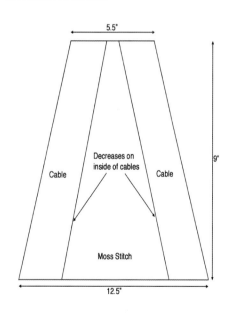

5.5"

Cable

Decreases on inside of cables

Cable

9"

Moss Stitch

12.5"

CHILL

SIZES
XS (to fit bust 32"/81cm)
S (to fit bust 34"/86cm)
M (to fit bust 36"/91cm)
L (to fit bust 38"/96cm)
XL (to fit bust 40"/101cm)
- see schematic for actual measurements.
Figures in parenthesis relate to S, M, L and XL sizes respectively. When there is only one figure, this relates to all.

YARN
ARTESANO Hummingbird: (327yds/300m per 150g hanks 3(4, 4, 4, 4) hanks PHEASANT

NEEDLES
3.25 mm (US 3) and 4 mm (US 6);
extra long 3.25mm circular needle;
or size to obtain tension, stitch holders. We recommend   Brittany Needles

NOTIONS
2 large buttons

TENSION
22 sts and 28 rows = 4"/10 cms over st st. Please work swatch and check carefully. If wrong alter size of needles until correct tension is achieved.

STITCHES
Garter Stitch
Knit every row
2 x 2 rib
RS rows   k2, *p2, k2; rep from * to end
WS rows   p2, *k2, p2: rep from * to end **Stitch pattern** Rows 1, 3, 5, 7, 9, 11 & 12 Knit
Rows 2, 4, 6, 8 & 10 Purl
Repeat these 12 rows

BACK
Using smaller straight needles, cast on 90(96, 102, 108, 114) sts.
Work 4 rows in garter st, then change to larger needles and refer to Stitch Pattern above and repeat to end, dec 1st at both ends of every 7th row 0(0, 2, 0, 0) times, then every 8th row 2(2, 3, 3, 3) times, then ev 9th row 2(2, 0, 2, 2) times – 82(88, 92, 98, 94) sts. Cont in patt as set for 10 rows, then inc 1 st at both ends of next row, then as follows, keeping patt correct:
XS & S   ev foll 12th row three times – 90(96) sts
M   ev foll 8th row 4 times – 102 sts
L & XL   ev foll 7th

row 4 times – 108(114) sts
Cont in patt as set until work measures 13.5" [34.25 cm] from cast on edge ending on a WS row, **shape armhole:**
Cast off 4(5, 5, 6, 6) sts at beg of next 2 rows. Dec 1 st at both ends of next and ev foll alt row 5(6, 8, 9, 11) times in all, keeping patt correct – 72(74, 76, 78, 80)sts.
Cont until work measures 20.25(20.25, 20.75, 21.25, 21.25)")" [51.5(51.5, 52.75, 54, 54)cm] from cast on edge, ending on WS row, then **shape shoulder and neck:**
Ne xt row (RS)   Work 22sts, place centre 28(30, 32, 34, 36) sts on holder, join a second ball of yarn and work to end. Working both sides at the same time, dec 1 st at both neck edges on next and foll alt row.
At the same time work and place 6 sts on holder at armhole edge on next row, (for left back neck it will be foll row), and 7 sts on foll **alternate** row. Cast off over all 20sts.

LEFT FRONT
Using smaller straight needles, cast on 34(36, 38, 42, 44) sts.
Work 4 rows in garter st, then change to larger needles and refer to Stitch Pattern above and repeat to end, dec 1st at armhole edge of every 7th row 0(0,

2, 0, 0) times, then every 8th row 2(2, 3, 3, 3) times, then ev 9th row 2(2, 0, 2, 2) times – 30(32, 33, 37, 39) sts. Cont in patt as set for 10 rows, then inc 1 st at armhole edge of next row, then as follows, keeping pattt correct:
XS & S   ev foll 12th row three times – 34(36) sts
M   ev foll 8th row 4 times – 38 sts
L & XL   ev foll 7th row 4 times – 42(44) sts
Cont in patt as set until work measures 12(12, 12.5, 13, 13)" [30.5(30.5, 31.75, 33, 33) cm] ending on RS row and then **shape neckline:**
Dec 1 st at beg of next, then dec as foll:
XS, S & M at neck edge ev foll 13th row 4 times
L & XL   at neck edge ev foll 8th row 6 times
At the same time when work measures 13.5" [34.25 cm] from cast on edge ending on a WS row, **shape armhole:**
Cast off 4(5, 5, 6, 6) sts at beg of next row. Work 1 row, then dec 1 st at beg of next and ev foll alt row 5(6, 8, 9, 11) times in all, keeping patt correct.
Cont until work measures 20.25(20.25, 20.75, 21.25, 21.25)" [51.5(51.5, 52.75, 54, 54)cm] from cast on edge ending on WS row, then work shoulder:
Work and place 6 sts on

holder at armhole edge on next row, and 7 sts on foll **alt** row. Cast off over all 20 sts.

RIGHT FRONT
Work as for left front reversing all shapings.

SLEEVES
Using smaller straight needles, cast on 54(54, 58, 62, 62) sts.
Work 4" [10 cm] in 2 x 2 rib as above, then change to larger needles and refer to Stitch Pattern and repeat to end, starting on row 5(5, 7, 9, 9) so that pattern matches at armhole, inc as foll, keeping patt correct as set:
XS   1 st at both ends of ev 28th row 3 times – 60 sts
S   1 st at both ends of ev 22nd row 4 times – 62 sts
M   1 st at both ends of ev 14th row 6 times – 70 sts
L   1 st at both ends of ev 14th row 6 times – 74 sts
XL   1 st at both ends of ev 10th row 4 times, then ev 11th row 4 times – 78 sts
Cont in patt as set until work measures 18(18, 18.25, 18.5, 18.5)" [45.75(45.75, 46.5, 47, 47)cm] from cast on edge ending on WS row and then **shape sleeve cap:**
Cast off 4(5, 5, 6, 6) sts at beg of next 2 rows. Then dec 1 st at both ends of ev 3rd row 2(4, 2, 2, 0) times, then ev alt row 13(10, 14,

15, 18) times – 22(24, 28, 28, 30)sts.
Cast off 2 sts at beg of next 4 rows,. Cast off rem 14(16, 20, 20, 22) sts

FINISHING
Use a small neat backstitch on edge of work for all seams except cuffs, where an invisible slip stitch should be used. Join shoulder seams.

BAND
Using circular needle but working back and forth, with RS facing, starting at right front bottom edge, pick up and k80(81, 84, 89, 90) sts up right front to neck shap-

ing, k67 sts up sloping neck edge to shoulder, k2 sts down right back neck edge, k28(30, 32, 34, 36) sts from holder at centre back, k2 sts up left back neck edge, k67 sts down sloping edge of left neck and k80(81, 84, 89, 90) sts down to bottom left front – 326(330, 338, 350, 354) sts. Work 4.5" [11.5 cm] in 2 x 2 rib, starting on a WS row.

At the same time when work measures 2.75" [7 cm] ending on WS row, work 2 **buttonholes:**
Work 76(76, 80, 84, 84) sts, turn and work 6 rows on these sts and then leave on

holder. Rejoin yarn and work 12(12, 12, 14, 14) sts, turn and work 6 further rows, then leave these sts on holder. Rejoin yarn and work 7 rows on the remaining sts.

Next row Work across all sts
Cont until work measures 4.5" [11.5 cm] and then cast off loosely in rib on RS row. Insert sleeves placing any fullness evenly over top of sleeve cap. Join side and sleeve seams in one line. Sew two buttons on left band to correspond with buttonholes.

● ● ● ●

CHILL SCHEMATIC

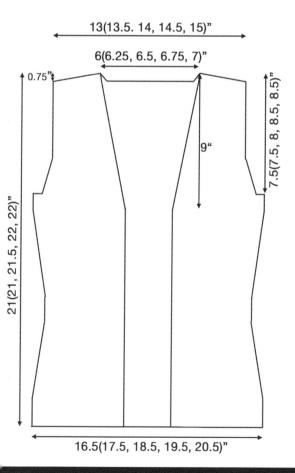

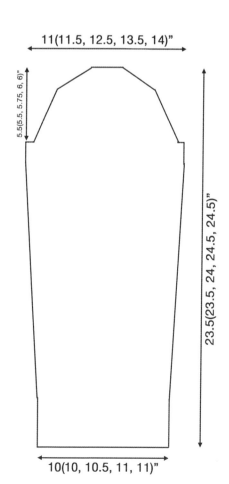

BOP

SIZES

XS (to fit bust 32"/81cm)
S (to fit bust 34"/86cm)
M (to fit bust 36"/91cm)
L (to fit bust 38"/96cm)
XL (to fit bust 40"/101cm)
- see schematic for actual measurements.
Figures in parenthesis relate to S, M, L and XL sizes respectively. When there is only one figure, this relates to all.

YARN

ARTESANO Hummingbird: (327yds/100m per 150g hank):3(4, 4, 5, 5) hanks LOVEBIRD

NEEDLES

3.75 mm (US 5) and 4.5 mm (US 7); or size to obtain tension, stitch holders. We recomend Brittany Needles.

NOTIONS

2/3 lengths of 72" [2m] x 0.375" [10mm] velvet/satin ribbon

TENSION

20 sts and 26 rows = 4"/10 cms over st st. Please work swatch and check carefully. If wrong alter size of needles until correct tension is achieved.

STITCHES

Garter Stitch
Knit every row
Stocking Stitch
Knit on RS and purl on WS rows

BACK & FRONT

(both alike to armholes)
Using smaller needles cast on 120(128, 136, 142, 150) sts. Work 6 rows in garter st, then change to larger needles and cont in st st until work measures 21" [53.5 cm] from cast on edge ending on WS row.

Next row

XS (k1, k2tog) across row – 80 sts

S (k1, k2tog) across row to last 2 sts, k2 – 86 sts

M (k2tog, k1) across row to last 4 sts, k2tog, k2tog – 90 sts

L k1, (k1, k2tog) across row to last 3 sts, k3 – 96 sts

XL (k1, k2tog) across row – 100 sts.

Next row Knit
Change to smaller needles an work first eyelet row:

XS & S k1, (yarn over needle to make a st (yo), k2tog) across row to last st, k1

M & L k2, (yarn over needle to make a st (yo), k2tog) across row to last st, k1

XL k1, (yarn over needle to make a st (yo), k2tog) across row

Next row Purl
Work two more eyelet rows by repeating the last 2 rows once, then the first row again. Then knit 1 row. Cast off.
Using larger needles, with RS facing, pick up and k80(86, 90, 96, 100) sts across top of back/front. Purl 1 row and then cont in st st to end. When work measures 25.5(25.5, 25, 25.5, 25.5)" [64.75, 64.75, 63. 5, 64.75, 64.75 cm] from cast on edge ending on a WS row, **shape armhole:**

Cast off 5 sts at beg of next 2 rows. Dec 1 st at both ends of next and ev foll alt row 2(4, 5, 7, 8) times in all, keeping patt correct – 66(68, 70, 72, 74)sts.

Back neck shaping
Cont until work measures 31(31, 31, 32, 32)" [78.75(78.75, 78.75, 81.25, 81.25)cm] from cast on edge, ending on WS row, work back neck:

Next row (RS) Work 19(20, 19, 20, 21)sts, cast off centre 28(28, 32, 32, 32) sts, work to end. Join a second ball of yarn and work both sides at the same time, dec 1 st at both neck edges on next ev foll row 8 times – 11(12, 11, 12, 13) sts.

Cont until work measures 32.25(32.25, 32.25, 33.25, 33.25)" [82(82, 82, 84.5, 84.5)cm] from cast on edge ending on WS row, then work shoulders:

Work and place 6 sts on holder at armhole edge on next row, (for left back neck it will be foll row), and 5(6, 5, 6, 7) sts on foll **alternate** row. Cast off over all 11(12, 11, 12, 13) sts.

Front neck shaping
At the same time as armhole shaping, when work measures 25.5(25.5, 25.5, 26, 26)" [64.75(64.75, 64.75, 66, 66)cm] from cast on edge ending on WS row, commence front neck:
Next row (RS)   Work 25(28, 23, 26, 27)sts, cast off centre 30(30, 32, 32, 34) sts, work to end. Join a second ball of yarn and work both sides at the same time, dec as foll:
1 st at both neck edges on next, then ev foll 3rd row 0(0, 3, 1, 0) times, then ev foll 4th row 5(5, 4, 6, 3) times, then ev foll 5th row 1(1, 0, 0, 3) times – 11(12, 11, 12, 13) sts.
Cont until work measures

32.25(32.25, 32.25, 33.25, 33.25)" [82(82, 82, 84.5, 84.5)cm] from cast on edge ending on WS row, then work shoulders:
Work and place 6 sts on holder at armhole edge on next row, (for left back neck it will be foll row), and 5(6, 5, 6, 7) sts on foll **alternate** row. Cast off over all 11(12, 11, 12, 13) sts.

FINISHING
Use a small neat backstitch on edge of work for all seams except welts, where an invisible slip stitch should be used. Join right shoulder seam.

Neckline edging
With right side facing, using smaller needles and starting at left shoulder, pick up and k18(18, 18, 20, 20) sts down straight front neck, k20(20, 20, 22, 22) sts down sloping neck edge, k28(28, 30, 30, 32) sts across centre front, k20(20, 20, 22, 22) sts up sloping right front edge, k18(18, 18, 20, 20) sts up straight side of right neck edge, k10 sts down right back neck, k24(24, 28, 28, 28) sts across centre back and 10 sts up left neck edge – 148(148, 154, 162, 164) sts. Knit 3 rows and then cast off using picot point cast-off:
Picot point cast off
Cast off 2 sts, *slip rem st

on RH needle onto LH needle, cast on 2 sts, cast off 4 sts; repeat from * to end and fasten off rem st.
Join left shoulder seam. Insert sleeves placing any fullness evenly over top of sleeve cap.

Armhole edging
With right side facing, using smaller needles, pick up and k75(75, 80, 85, 85) sts around armhole edge. Knit 3 rows, then cast off using picot point cast-off as above.

Join side and sleeve seams in one line.

Thread two or three (according to preference) lengths of ribbon through eyelets below bust and either join each one on inside at side seam or tie at centre front or back on outside.

SCHEMATIC

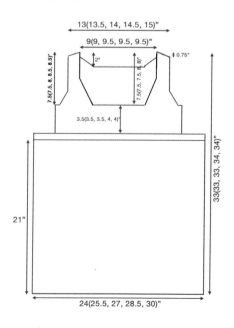

Rapt

SIZES

One size – 31.5" [80 cm]
long x 74" [188 cm] wide
(including edging)
- see schematic.

YARN

ARTESANO Hummingbird:
(327yds/300m per 150g
hank):
4 hanks STARLING

NEEDLES

Pair extra long 5 mm (US
8); 2 x 4mm (US 6) double
pointed needles (dpns), or
size to obtain tension; stitch
holder; tapestry needle. We
recommend Brittany Needles

TENSION

20 sts and 26 rows = 4"/10
cms over st st. Please work
swatch and check carefully.
If wrong alter size of needles until correct tension is
achieved.

STITCHES

Slip the first stitch and knit
into the back of the last
stitch on every row. This
creates a notched edge on
which to attach the knit-on
border.

Stocking Stitch

RS rows   Knit
WS rows   Purl

CENTRE TRIANGLE

Using 5mm (US 8) needles,
cast on 6 sts. Work 4 rows
in st st.
Next row(RS)   k3, wool
round needle to make a
stitch (wrn), k3 – 7 sts
Next row   p3, wrn, p1,
wrn, p3 – 9 sts
Next row   k3, wrn, k3,
wrn, k3 – 11 sts
Next row   p3, wrn, p5,
wrn, p3 – 13 sts
Next row   k3, wrn, k7,
wrn, k3 – 15 sts
Next row   p3, wrn, p9,
wrn, p3 – 17 sts
Next row   k3, wrn, k11,
wrn, k3 – 19 sts
Cont as above, keeping pattern correct, increasing 1 st
on both sides, three sts in on
every row. When there are
351 sts, place sts on holder.

BORDER NB Use back-
wards loop cast on.

Make a backwards loop and
place it on the needle.
Repeat until you have as
many stitches as you re-
quire.
Using two 4 mm (US 6) dpns
and smooth waste yarn in
contrasting colour, cast on 8
sts and work 3 rows.
Next row   p8 in contrast
colour, then cast on 20 sts
in main yarn. Cont in main
yarn and work border as
below as foll:
Start at centre of top of
shawl, working into every
stitch. Knit on the edging as
you go, at end of every second border row.
NB   Single join is working
once into one selvedge hole
(space between two
notches on edge), or one st
along top edge - 2 rows
Double join is working twice
into one selvedge hole
(space between two notches
on edge), or one st along
top edge - 4 rows
Join the border to the shawl
using single and double joins
by working together one
stitch from the top edge with
the last stitch on WS rows.
On sloping edges work as
schematic, working four
double joins at each end,
then for 81 selvedge spaces
between work as follows:
*pick up 1 st and then cast
off 1 st into one selvedge
space(one space = 2 rows),
then pick up 1 st, cast off 1
st twice into following selvedge space, matching RS to
RS. Repeat from *, ending
with single join.
Row 1 (RS)   cast off
20, knit to end
Row 2   k3, p5
Row 3   knit
Row 4 & 8   *wrn,
k2tog, rep from * to end
Row 5, 7, 9 & 11   knit

Rows 6 & 10   k3, p5
Row 12   *wrn, k2tog, rep
from * 3 times more, cast on
20 sts
Row 13   cast off 20 sts,
k8
Row 14   k3, p5
Rows 15, 17 & 19 knit
Row 16   *wrn, k2tog, rep
from * to end
Row 18   k3, p5
Row 20   *wrn, k2tog,
rep from * to end, then turn
up the first unattached cord
of knitting and knit into the
first cast off stitch to attach
it. **NB Take care that the
cord isn't twisted.**
Row 21   k2tog, k
to end
Row 22   k3, p5
Row 23   knit

Rep rows 12-23 44 more
times around edge of shawl,
making double joins in plac-
es indicated on schematic ie
first four and last four spaces
down sloping edges.

FINISHING
Place 8 sts on waste yarn at
beg of edging on needle.
Using **Kitchener st,** graft
together the start and finish
of edging:
Hold the two needles parallel
close together with the yarn
coming from the RH end
of the back needle. Break
your yarn leaving a 10" end.
Thread it onto a tapestry
needle.
1   Bring yarn through the
first stitch on front needle as

if to knit, and slip the
stitch off the knitting needle
2   Bring yarn through the
second stitch of front needle
as if to   purl, and leave
the stitch on the knitting
needle
3   Bring yarn through the
first stitch of back needle
as if to purl, and slip the
stitch off the knitting needle
4   Bring yarn through
the second stitch of the back
needle as if to knit and leave
it on.
Repeat from 1 - 4 until all
stitches are used up. Weave
in end and snip off.
Sew in place one remaining
cord of knitting, keeping
pattern correct.

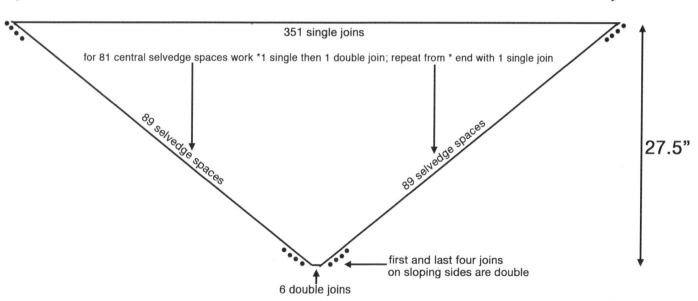

70" (without edging)

351 single joins

for 81 central selvedge spaces work *1 single then 1 double join; repeat from * end with 1 single join

89 selvedge spaces

89 selvedge spaces

27.5"

first and last four joins
on sloping sides are double

6 double joins

• Double join

Except where indicated all other joins are single

CHRYSALIS

SIZES

XS (to fit bust 32"/81cm)
S (to fit bust 34"/86cm)
M (to fit bust 36"/91cm)
L (to fit bust 38"/96cm)
XL (to fit bust 40"/101cm)
- see schematic for actual measurements. Figures in parenthesis relate to S, M, L and XL sizes respectively. When there is only one figure, this relates to all.

YARN

ARTESANO Hummingbird:
(327yds/300m per 150g hank):
3 hanks LOVEBIRD

NEEDLES

3.75 mm (US 5) and 4 mm (US 6); or size to obtain tension. We recommend Brittany Needles

TENSION

22 sts and 28 rows = 4"/10 cms over st st. Please work swatch and check carefully. If wrong alter size of needles until correct tension is achieved.

STITCHES

Stocking St   Knit every RS row and purl every WS row
Lacy Rib   Multiple of 4 + 1
Row 1(RS)   k1, *p3, k1; rep from * to end
Row 2   p1,   *k3, p1; rep from * to end
Row 3   as Row 1
Row 4   as Row 2
Row 5   k1, *p2tog, yrn (yarn around needle to make a st), p1, k1; rep from * to end
Row 6   as Row 2
Repeat these 6 rows

BACK

Using smaller needles, cast on 93(97, 105, 109, 117) sts. Work 8 rows in Lacy Rib Stitch (6 row repeat, plus first 2 rows).
Change to larger needles and cont in st st, dec 1st at both ends of every 5th row twice, then every 6th row 3(3, 3, 4, 4) times – 83(87, 95, 97, 95) sts. Cont in st st for 10 rows, then inc 1 st st both ends of next, then ev foll 4th row 0(0, 0, 2, 2) times, then ev 5th row 3(3, 3, 3, 3) times, then ev 6th row 1(1, 1, 0, 0) times - 93(97, 105, 109, 117) sts. Cont in st st until work measures 10(10, 10.5, 11, 11)" [25.5(25.5, 26.75, 28, 28)cm] from cast on edge ending on a WS row, then change to Lacy Rib and repeat to end.

When work measures 13.5" [34.25cm] from cast on edge, ending on WS row, **shape armhole:**
Cast off 5 sts at beg of next 2 rows. Dec 1 st at both ends of next and ev foll alt row 5(5, 9, 9, 12) times, keeping lacy rib pattern correct – 73(77, 77, 81, 83)sts. Cont until work measures 20.25(20.25, 20.75, 21.25, 21.25)")" [51.5(51.5, 52.75, 54, 54)cm] then **shape shoulder and neck:**
Next row (RS)   Work 18(18, 17, 19, 17)sts, place centre 37(41, 43, 43, 49) sts on holder, join a second ball of yarn and work to end. Working both sides at the same time, dec 1 st at both neck edges on next and foll alt row.
At the same time work and place 5 sts on holder at armhole edge on next row, (for left back neck it will be foll row), and 5(5, 5, 6, 5) sts on foll **alternate** row. Cast off over all 16(16, 15, 17, 15)sts.

FRONT

Work as for back until work measures 14.5(14.5, 15, 15, 15)" [36.75(36.75, 38, 38, 38)cm] from cast on edge ending on a WS row, then **work neckline (whilst cont with armhole shaping):**
Next row Work to centre st, place this on holder, join

a second ball of yarn and work to end. Working both sides at the same time and keeping lacy rib correct, work as follows:

XS Cast off 2 sts at neck edge on next 14 rows, then inc 1 st at neck edge on foll 3rd row 4 times, then foll 4th row 4 times – 16 sts.

S Cast off 2 sts at neck edge on next 12 rows, then 3 sts at neck edge on foll 2 rows, then inc 1 st at neck edge on foll 3rd row 4 times, then on foll 4th row 4 times – 16sts.

M Cast off 2 sts at neck edge on next 12 rows, then 3 sts at neck edge on foll 2 rows, then inc 1 st at neck edge on foll 4th row 7 times – 15sts

L Cast off 2 sts at neck edge on next 16 rows, then inc 1 st at neck edge on foll 3rd row 6 times, then foll 4th row 3 times – 17 sts.

XL Cast off 2 sts at neck edge on next 15 rows, then 3 sts at neck edge on foll row, then inc 1 st at neck edge on foll 4th row 5 times, then foll 5th row twice – 15 sts.

Cont until work measures 20.25(20.25, 20.75, 21.25, 21.25)" [51.5(51.5, 52.75, 54, 54)cm] ending on WS row, then work shoulder: Work and place 5 sts on holder at armhole edge on

next row, (for right front neck it will be foll row), and 5(5, 5, 6, 5) sts on foll **alt** row. Cast off over all 16(16, 15, 17, 15)sts.

SLEEVES

Using smaller needles, cast on 93(93, 101, 109, 113) sts. Work 37(37, 37, 41, 41) rows in **Lacy Rib.**

Next row (WS):   p1, *k1, k2tog, p1; rep from * to end - 70(70, 76, 82, 85) sts

Change to larger needles and cont in st st to end, dec 9(7, 7, 7, 8)sts evenly across first row – 61(63, 69, 75, 77) sts. Cont until work measures 12(12, 12.5, 12.5, 12.5)" [30.5(30.5, 31.75, 31.75, 31.75)cm] from cast on edge ending on WS row and then **shape sleeve cap:**

Cast off 5 sts at beg of next 2 rows. Then dec 1 st at both ends of ev 3rd row 4(4, 0, 0, 0) times, then ev alt row 10(10, 16, 17, 17) times, then ev row 0(0, 0, 2, 2) times – 23(25, 27, 27, 29)sts.

Cast off 2 sts at beg of next 4 rows,. Cast off rem 15(17, 19, 19, 21) sts

FINISHING

Use a small neat backstitch on edge of work for all seams except cuffs, where an invisible slip stitch should be used. Join right shoulder seam. Then using smaller needles, with RS facing, pick up and k26(26, 26, 28, 28) sts down left front neck edge, k32(34, 36, 36, 38) sts down to centre front, k1 st from holder at centre front, k32(34, 36, 36, 38) sts up right front neck to corner, k26(26, 26, 28, 28) sts to right shoulder seam, 2 sts down right back neck, k37(41, 43, 43, 49) sts from holder at centre back and 2 sts up left back neck – 158(166, 172, 176, 186) sts. Knit 1 row and then cast off knitwise.   Join left shoulder seam. Insert sleeves placing any fullness evenly over top of sleeve cap. Join side and sleeve seams in one line.

SCHEMATIC

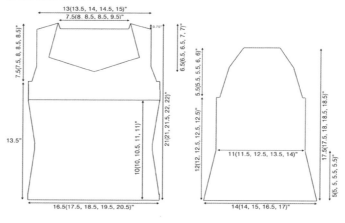

TWISTER

SIZES
One size 60" [152.5 cm] long and 6" [15.25 cm] wide - see schematic

YARN
ARTESANO Hummingbird: (327yds/300m per 150g hank):
1 hank LOURIE

NEEDLES
4 mm (US 6); or size to obtain tension
stitch holders
We recommend Brittany Needles

TENSION
24 sts and 28 rows = 4"/10 cms over 2 x 2 rib. Please work swatch and check carefully. If wrong alter size of needles until correct tension is achieved.

STITCHES
2 x 2 Rib
Multiple of 4
Row 1   *k2, p2, rep from * to end
Repeat row 1 throughout

TO MAKE SCARF
First half
Cast on 20 sts and work in 2 x 2 rib as above to end. When 10 rows are completed, cont as foll:
**Next row   Work 14 sts and place rem 6 sts on holder.
Cont in these 14 sts in patt as set for a further 13 rows and then place these sts on 2nd holder. Do not cut yarn. Slip 6 sts from first holder to needle, join new ball of yarn and work 20 rows, keeping patt correct as set. Cut yarn and place sts on first holder.
Second half
Cast on 20 sts and work in 2 x 2 to end. When 10 rows are completed, cont as foll:
Work 6 sts, place rem 14 sts on 3rd holder. Work 20 rows, keeping patt correct as set. Do not cut yarn and place sts on 4th holder.
Slip 14 sts from 3rd holder onto needle, join new ball of yarn and patt to end. work 14 rows in patt as set. Break yarn and place on 3rd holder.
Next row   Patt 14 sts from first half -2nd holder, twist the two middle strips around each other as in Diagram 1, then patt 6 sts from first half - 1st holder, then using the ball attached to second strip, patt 6 sts from second half – 4th holder, then patt 14 sts from second half - 3rd holder.

Working the 20 sts of each half separately, cont in patt as set for 7 rows. **
Repeat from ** to ** until scarf measures approximately 60" [152.5 cm], ending on a full repeat. Work a further 2 rows in patt, then cast off each half separately.

FINISHING
Weave in loose ends securely.

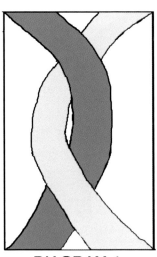

DIAGRAM 1

SCHEMATIC

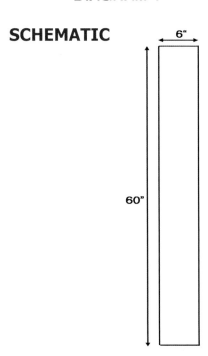

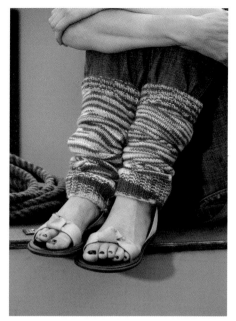

JAZZ

SIZES
S, M & L – see schematic for actual sizes

YARN
ARTESANO Hummingbird: (327yds/300m per 150g hank):
1(1, 2) hanks WOODPECKER

NEEDLES
One pair 3.75mm needles (US 5)
One pair 4mm (US 6)
or size to obtain tension
We recommend Brittany Needles

22 sts and 28 rows = 4"/10 cms over st st. Please work swatch and check carefully. If wrong alter size of needles until correct tension is achieved.

STITCHES
2 x 2 Rib
Multiple of 4
Row 1 (RS) p1, *k2, p2, rep from * to last 3 sts, k2, p1
Row 2   k1, *p2, k2, rep from * to last 3 sts, p2, k1
Repeat these 2 rows
Stocking Stitch
RS rows   Knit
WS rows   Purl

LEGWARMER
Make two.

Using smaller needles cast on 56(60, 64) sts and work 20 rows in 2 x 2 rib. Change to larger needles and working in st st, inc 1 st as follows:
S   at both ends of 17th, then ev 18th row 5 times in all – 66 sts.
M   at both ends of 15th, then ev 14th row 6 times in all – 72 sts.
L   at both ends of 15th, then ev 14th row 6 times in all – 76 sts.

Inc rows   k3, knit into front and back of next st to make 1 st (m1), knit to last 4 sts, m1 in next st, k3

Cont until work measures 17.5" [44.5 cm] from cast on edge ending on a WS row, then change to smaller needles and work 12 rows in 2 x 2 rib. Cast off in rib.

MAKING UP
Press pieces on wrong side. Join seams with a small backstitch on very edge of work, taking care not to pull too tight.

JAZZ SCHEMATIC

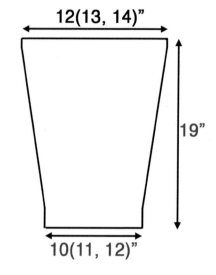

12(13, 14)"

19"

10(11, 12)"

SNUG

SIZES

XS (to fit bust 32")
S (to fit bust 34")
M (to fit bust 36")
L (to fit bust 38")
XL (to fit bust 42")
- see schematic for actual measurements. Figures in parenthesis relate to S, M, L and XL sizes respectively. When there is only one figure, this relates to all.

YARN

ARTESANO Hummingbird: (327yds/300m per 150g hank):
2(3, 3, 3, 3) hanks TURTLEDOVE

NEEDLES

3.25 mm (US 3) and 4 mm (US 6);
extra long 3.25mm circular needle;
or size to obtain tension, cable needle; stitch holders
We recommend Brittany Needles

TENSION

22 sts and 28 rows = 4"/10 cms over st st. Please work swatch and check carefully. If wrong alter size of needles until correct tension is achieved.

STITCHES

Slip the first stitch and knit into the back of the last stitch on every row.

Moss (or Seed) Stitch

Row 1   *k1, p1; repeat from * to end
Row 2   Knit the purl sts and purl the knit stitches
Repeat row 2

Stocking Stitch

RS rows   Knit
WS rows   Purl

Picot point cast off

Cast off 2 sts, *slip rem st on RH needle onto LH needle, cast on 2 sts, cast off 4 sts; repeat from * to end and fasten off rem st.

Glossary

C4b   place 2 sts on cable needle (cn) and hold at back of work, k2, k2 from cn
yf   yarn forward and around needle to make a stitch

BACK

Using smaller needles cast on 90(96, 102, 108, 114)sts and work 6 rows in moss st. Change to larger needles and cont in st st to end, dec 1st at both ends of every 7th row 0(0, 2, 0, 0) times, then every 8th row 2(2, 3, 3, 3) times, then ev 9th row 2(2, 0, 2, 2) times – 82(88, 92, 98, 94) sts. Cont in patt as set for 10 rows, then inc 1 st at both ends of next row, then as follows, keeping patt correct:
XS & S   ev foll 12th row three times – 90(96) sts
M   ev foll 8th row 4 times – 102 sts
L & XL   ev foll 7th row 4 times – 108(114) sts
Cont in patt as set until work measures 13.5" [34.25 cm] from cast on edge ending on a WS row, **shape armhole:**
Cast off 4(5, 5, 6, 6) sts at beg of next 2 rows. Dec 1 st at both ends of next and ev foll alt row 5(6, 8, 9, 11) times in all, keeping patt correct – 72(74, 76, 78, 80)sts. Cont until work measures 20.25(20.25, 20.75, 21.25, 21.25)")" [51.5(51.5, 52.75, 54, 54)cm] from cast on edge, ending on WS row, then **shape shoulder and neck:**
Next row (RS)   Work 22sts, cast off centre 28(30, 32, 34, 36) sts, join a second ball of yarn and work to end. Working both sides at the same time, dec 1 st at both neck edges on next and foll alt row.
At the same time work and place 6 sts on holder at armhole edge on next row, (for left back neck it will be foll row), and 7 sts on foll **alternate** row. Cast off over all 20sts.

LEFT FRONT

Using smaller straight needles cast on 72(76, 80, 84, 88)sts. Work 6 rows in moss st, then change to larger needles and cont in st st with lacy cable at centre front, repeating the foll 6 rows to end:

Row 1 (RS) k to last 10 sts, p3, k4, p3

Row 2 k1, yf, k2tog, p4, k1, yf, k2tog, p to end

Row 3 k to last 10 sts, p3, C4b, p3

Row 4 as Row 2

Row 5 as Row 1

Row 6 as Row 2

At the same time dec 1st at armhole edge of every 7th row 0(0, 2, 0, 0) times, then every 8th row 2(2, 3, 3, 3) times, then ev 9th row 2(2, 0, 2, 2) times – 68(72, 75, 79, 83) sts. Cont in patt as set for 10 rows, then inc 1 st at armhole edge of next row, then as follows, keeping patt correct:

XS & S ev foll 12th row three times – 72(76) sts

M ev foll 8th row 4 times – 80 sts

L & XL ev foll 7th row 4 times – 84(88) sts

At the same time when work measures 6(6. 6.5, 6.5, 6.5)" [15.25(15.25, 16.5, 16.5, 16.5) cm] ending on RS row, **shape neckline:**

Next row Work 10 sts in patt as set, dec 1 st, work to end. Cont to dec in this way

10 sts in from centre front edge ev alt row 8(14, 20, 22, 28)times in all, then ev 3rd row 25(21, 17, 17, 13) times.

At the same time when work measures 13.5" [34.25 cm] from cast on edge ending on a WS row, **shape armhole:**

Cast off 4(5, 5, 6, 6) sts at beg of next row. Work 1 row, then dec 1 st at beg of next and ev foll alt row 5(6, 8, 9, 11) times in all, keeping patt correct.

Cont until work measures 20.25(20.25, 20.75, 21.25, 21.25)" [51.5(51.5, 52.75, 54, 54)cm] from cast on edge ending on WS row, then **work shoulder:**

Work and place 6 sts on holder at armhole edge on next row, and 7 sts on foll alt row. Cast off over 20 shoulder sts, leaving 10 sts at neck edge on holder.

RIGHT FRONT

Work as for Left Front reversing all shapings and lacy rib pattern at centre front edge. Cast off the lace rib edging on last row of shoulder shaping.

FINISHING

Use small neat backstitch for all seams except welts where an edge to edge slip stitch should be used. Join left shoulder seam. Then using

larger needles, pick up 10 sts on holder at left shoulder and continue in lacy cable patt until the band will reach right shoulder seam when stretched. **NB** It is important that there is no excess here as the neck should fit snugly. Slip stitch the band in place as you knit and cast off when the band fits snugly when stretched slightly, with no puckering. **Join right shoulder seam.**

Neckband edging

Using circular needle, but working back and forth, with right side facing, starting at bottom right centre front, pick up and k32(32, 34, 34, 34) sts to start of neck shaping, k86(86, 86, 92, 92) sts to right shoulder seam, k32(34, 34, 36, 36) sts across back neck and k86(86, 86, 92, 92) sts down left front sloping neck edge, and k32(32, 34, 34, 34) sts down straight edge of left front to bottom edge – 268(270, 274, 288, 288)sts. Purl 1 row, then cast off using picot point cast off.

Armbands

Using smaller needles, with RS facing, pick up and k84(84, 90, 96, 96)sts evenly around armhole edge.

SNUG CONT.

Work 3 rows in moss st and then cast off using **picot point cast off.**

Ties

Make 2

Using smaller needles, cast on 7 sts and work in moss st until work measures 38" [96.5cm] and then cast off. Attach to gilet along straight edge below neck shaping, beneath picot edging.

Join side seams in one line leaving 1" [2.5 cm] space (to fit tie) in right side seam at waist.

SNUG SCHEMATIC

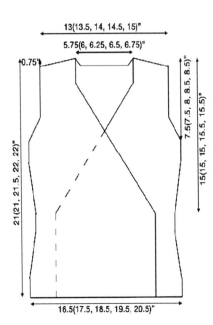

HUG

SIZES

XS (to fit bust 32")
S (to fit bust 34")
M (to fit bust 36")
L (to fit bust 38")
XL (to fit bust 42")
- see schematic for actual measurements. Figures in parenthesis relate to S, M, L and XL sizes respectively. When there is only one figure, this relates to all.

YARN

ARTESANO Hummingbird dk: (327yds/300m per 150g hank):
3(3, 4, 4, 4) hanks
FLAMINGO

NEEDLES

3.25 mm (US 3) and 4 mm (US 6);
extra long 3.25mm circular needle;
or size to obtain tension, cable
needle; stitch holders.
We recommend Brittany Needles

TENSION

22 sts and 28 rows = 4"/10 cms over st st. Please work swatch and check carefully. If wrong alter size of needles until correct tension is achieved.

STITCHES

Slip the first stitch and knit into the back of the last stitch on every row.

Moss (or Seed) Stitch

Row 1   *k1, p1; repeat from *   to end
Row 2   Knit the purl sts and purl the knit stitches
Repeat row 2

Stocking Stitch

RS rows   Knit
WS rows   Purl

Picot point cast off

Cast off 2 sts, *slip rem st on RH needle onto LH needle, cast on 2 sts, cast off 4 sts; repeat from * to end and fasten off rem st.

Glossary

C4b   place 2 sts on cable needle (cn) and hold at back of work, k2, k2 from cn
yf   yarn forward and around needle to make a stitch

BACK

Using smaller needles cast on 90(96, 102, 108, 114)sts and work 6 rows in moss st. Change to larger needles and cont in st st to end, dec 1st at both ends of every 7th row 0(0, 2, 0, 0) times, then every 8th row 2(2, 3, 3, 3) times, then ev 9th row 2(2, 0, 2, 2) times – 82(88, 92, 98, 94) sts. Cont in patt as set for 10 rows, then inc 1 st at both ends of next row, then as follows, keeping patt correct:

hug Page 1 of 4

XS & S   ev foll 12th row three times – 90(96) sts
M   ev foll 8th row 4 times – 102 sts
L & XL   ev foll 7th row 4 times – 108(114) sts
Cont in patt as set until work measures 13.5" [34.25 cm] from cast on edge ending on a WS row, **shape armhole:**
Cast off 4(5, 5, 6, 6) sts at beg of next 2 rows. Dec 1 st at both ends of next and ev foll alt row 5(6, 8, 9, 11) times in all, keeping patt correct – 72(74, 76, 78, 80)sts. Cont until work measures 20.25(20.25, 20.75, 21.25, 21.25)")" [51.5(51.5, 52.75, 54, 54)cm] from cast on edge, ending on WS row, then **shape shoulder and neck:**

Next row (RS)   Work 22sts, cast off centre 28(30, 32, 34, 36) sts, join a second ball of yarn and work to end. Working both sides at the same time, dec 1 st at both neck edges on next and foll alt row.

At the same time work and place 6 sts on holder at armhole edge on next row, (for left back neck it will be

foll row), and 7 sts on foll **alternate** row. Cast off over all 20sts.

LEFT FRONT
Using smaller straight needles cast on 72(76, 80, 84, 88)sts. Work 6 rows in moss st, then change to larger needles and cont in st st with lacy cable at centre front, repeating the foll 6 rows to end:
Row 1   (RS)   k to last 10 sts, p3, k4, p3
Row 2   k1, yf, k2tog, p4, k1, yf, k2tog, p to end
Row 3   k to last 10 sts, p3, C4b, p3
Row 4   as Row 2
Row 5   as Row 1
Row 6   as Row 2
At the same time dec 1st at armhole edge of every 7th row 0(0, 2, 0, 0) times, then every 8th row 2(2, 3, 3, 3) times, then ev 9th row 2(2, 0, 2, 2) times – 68(72, 75, 79, 83) sts. Cont in patt as set for 10 rows, then inc 1 st at armhole edge of next row, then as follows, keeping patt correct:
XS & S   ev foll 12th row three times – 72(76) sts
M   ev foll 8th row 4 times – 80 sts
L & XL   ev foll 7th row 4 times – 84(88) sts
At the same time when work measures 6(6. 6.5, 6.5, 6.5)" [15.25(15.25, 16.5, 16.5, 16.5) cm] ending on

RS row, **shape neckline:**
Next row   Work 10 sts in patt as set, dec 1 st, work to end. Cont to dec in this way 10 sts in from centre front edge ev alt row 8(14, 20, 22, 28)times in all, then ev 3rd row 25(21, 17, 17, 13) times.
At the same time when work measures 13.5" [34.25 cm] from cast on edge ending on a WS row, **shape armhole:**
Cast off 4(5, 5, 6, 6) sts at beg of next row. Work 1 row, then dec 1 st at beg of next and ev foll alt row 5(6, 8, 9, 11) times in all, keeping patt correct.
Cont until work measures 20.25(20.25, 20.75, 21.25, 21.25)" [51.5(51.5, 52.75, 54, 54)cm] from cast on edge ending on WS row, then **work shoulder:**
Work and place 6 sts on holder at armhole edge on next row, and 7 sts on foll **alt** row. Cast off over 20 shoulder sts, leaving 10 sts at neck edge on holder.

RIGHT FRONT
Work as for Left Front reversing all shapings and lacy rib pattern at centre front edge. Cast off the lace rib edging on last row of shoulder shaping.
SLEEVES
Using smaller straight needles, cast on 52(52, 52, 56, 56)sts.

HUG CONT. Work 4 rows in moss st as above, then change to larger needles and cont in st st to end, inc as foll:

XS 1 st at both ends of next and ev foll 22nd row 4 times in all – 60 sts
S 1 st at both ends of next and foll 18th row 5 times in all– 62 sts
M & L 1 st at both ends of next, then ev foll 8th row 4 times, then ev foll 10th row 4 times – 70 (74) sts
XL 1 st at both ends of next, then ev 6th row 4 times, then ev 8th row 6 times – 78 sts
Cont in patt as set until work measures 12(12, 12.5, 12.5, 12.5)" [30.5(30.5, 31.75, 31.75, 31.75)cm] from cast on edge ending on WS row and then **shape sleeve cap:**

Cast off 4(5, 5, 6, 6) sts at beg of next 2 rows. Then dec 1 st at both ends of ev 3rd row 2(4, 2, 2, 0) times, then ev alt row 13(10, 14, 15, 18) times – 22(24, 28, 28, 30)sts.
Cast off 2 sts at beg of next 4 rows,. Cast off rem 14(16, 20, 20, 22) sts

FINISHING
Use small neat backstitch for all seams except welts where an edge to edge slip stitch

should be used. Join left shoulder seam. Then using larger needles, pick up 10 sts on holder at left shoulder and continue in lacy cable patt until the band will reach right shoulder seam when stretched. NB It is important that there is no excess here as the neck should fit snugly. Slip stitch the band in place as you knit and cast off when the band fits snugly when stretched slightly, with no puckering. Join right shoulder seam.

Neckband edging
Using circular needle, but working back and forth, with right side facing, starting at bottom right centre front, pick up and k32(32, 34, 34, 34) sts to start of neck shaping, k86(86, 86, 92, 92) sts to right shoulder seam, k32(34, 34, 36, 36) sts across back neck and k86(86, 86, 92, 92) sts down left front sloping neck edge

and k32(32, 34, 34, 34) sts down straight edge of left front to bottom edge – 268(270, 274, 288, 288)sts. Purl 1 row, then cast off using picot point cast-off.

Ties,
Make 2
Using smaller needles, cast on 7 sts and work in moss st until work measures 38" [96.5cm] and then cast off. Attach to gilet along straight edge below neck shaping, beneath picot edging.

Sleeve edging
With right side facing, using smaller needles, pick up and k48(48, 48, 52, 52) sts along cuff edge. Purl 1 row and then cast off using picot point cast-off.
Insert sleeves, placing any fullness evenly over top of sleeve cap. Join side and sleeve seams in one line leaving 1" [2.5 cm] space (to fit tie) in right side seam at waist.

SCHEMATIC

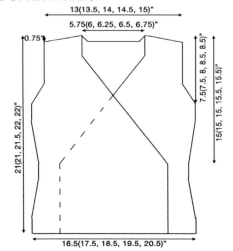

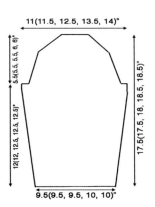

LACED

SIZES
XS, S, M, L, XL - finished length of belt without ties 22(24, 26, 28, 30)" [56(61, 66, 71, 76) cm]
Figures in parenthesis relate to S, M, L and XL sizes respectively. When there is only one figure, this relates to all.

YARN
ARTESANO Hummingbird: (327yds/300m per 150g hank):
1 hank SUNBIRD

NEEDLES
One pair 4 mm (US 6)
One pair 3.25 mm (US 3) or size to obtain tension
We recommend Brittany Needles

TENSION
20 sts and 36 rows = 4"/10 cms over st. Please work swatch and check carefully. If wrong alter size of needles until correct tension is achieved.

STITCHES
Moss (or Seed) Stitch
Row 1   *k1, p1; repeat from *   to end
Row 2   Knit the purl sts and purl the knit stitches. Repeat row 2

2 x 2 Rib
Multiple of 4
Row 1 (RS) k1, *p2, k2, rep from * to last 3 sts, p2, k1
Row 2   p1, *k2, p2, rep from * to last 3 sts, k2, p1
Repeat these 2 rows

TO MAKE BELT
Using smaller needles cast on 20 sts and work 1.5" [4 cm] in 2 x 2 rib as above ending on RS row. Knit one row to form foldline, then starting on Row 1, work a further 1.5" [4 cm] in 2 x 2 rib ending on WS row. Change to larger needles and cont as foll:
Next row (RS)   k1,(p1, k1) 3 times, join a new ball of yarn and k1,(p1, k1) 3 times over next 7 sts, join a third ball of yarn and k1,(p1, k1) 3 times over the final group, inc 1 st on the final st to make the 7 sts – 21 sts. Work the three groups of 7 sts separately but simultaneously. Cont in moss st until until each strip measures 21(23, 25, 27, 29)" [53.5(58.5, 63.5, 68.5, 73.5) cm] (the extra is to accommodate the plaiting). Plait the belt to size. Work next row in 2 x 2 rib over all 21 sts, working last 2 sts together – 20 sts. Change to smaller needles and work 1.5" [4 cm] in 2 x 2 rib as above ending on RS row. Knit one row to form foldline, then starting on Row 1, work a further 1.5" [4 cm] in 2 x 2 rib as above. Cast off.

FINISHING
Fold back ribs and slipstitch in place on wrong side. Sew sides of ribs.

SCHEMATIC

PLAITING SEQUENCE
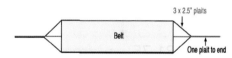

PLAITING CORDS, make 2
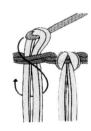

1. MEASURE OUT 3X3 LENGTHS OF YARN 60" (153CM)

2. ATTACH ONE SET OF YARN (AS IN DIAGRAM) TO THE TOPS AND THE BOTTOM EDGES OF THE RIB, WITH THE THIRD ONE IN THE MIDDLE, SO THAT WHEN ATTACHED EACH IS COMPRISED OF 6 STRANDS OF 30" (76.5CM)

3. USING 3 SETS OF 2 STRANDS, PLAIT EACH TIE UNTIL IT MEASURES 2.5" (6.5CM)

4. JOIN THREE TIES TOGETHER BY KNOTTING, THEN PLAITING 3 SETS OF 4 STRANDS (6 FROM REACH TIE) AND PLAIT TO 3" (7.5CM) FROM END.

5. KNOT THE CORD AGAIN, LEAVING A TASSLE OF APPROX 1.25" (3CM)

BOO

SIZES

XS (to fit bust 32"/81cm)
S (to fit bust 34"/86cm)
M (to fit bust 36"/91cm)
L (to fit bust 38"/96cm)
XL (to fit bust 40"/101cm)
- see schematic for actual measurements.
Figures in parenthesis relate to S, M, L and XL sizes respectively. When there is only one figure, this relates to all.

YARN

ARTESANO Hummingbird:
(327yds/300m per 150g hank):
4(4, 5, 5, 5) hanks
FLAMINGO

NEEDLES

3.75 mm (US 5) and 4.5 mm (US 7); or size to obtain tension, stitch holders.
We recommend Brittany Needles

NOTIONS

2/3 lengths of 72" [2m] x 0.375" [10mm] velvet/satin ribbon

BOO SCHEMATIC

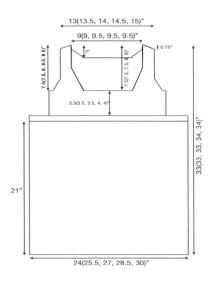

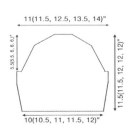

TENSION

20 sts and 26 rows = 4"/10 cms over st st. Please work swatch and check carefully. If wrong alter size of needles until correct tension is achieved.

STITCHES

Garter Stitch
Knit every row
Stocking Stitch
Knit on RS and purl on WS rows

BACK & FRONT

(both alike to armholes)
Using smaller needles cast on 120(128, 136, 142, 150) sts. Work 6 rows in garter st, then change to larger needles and cont in st st until work measures 21" [53.5 cm] from cast on edge ending on WS row.
Next row
XS (k1, k2tog) across row – 80 sts
S (k1, k2tog) across row to last 2 sts, k2 – 86 sts
M (k2tog, k1) across row to last 4 sts, k2tog, k2tog – 90 sts
L k1, (k1, k2tog) across row to last 3 sts, k3 – 96 sts
XL (k1, k2tog) across row – 100 sts.
Next row Knit
Change to smaller needles and work first eyelet row:
XS & S k1, (yarn over needle to make a st (yo), k2tog) across row to last st, k1
M & L k2, (yarn over needle to make a st (yo), k2tog) across row to last st, k1
XL k1, (yarn over needle to make a st (yo), k2tog) across row

Next row Purl
Work two more eyelet rows by repeating the last 2 rows once, then the first row again. Then knit 1 row.
Cast off.

Using larger needles, with RS facing, pick up and k80(86, 90, 96, 100) sts across top of back/front. Purl 1 row and then cont in st st to end. When work measures 25.5(25.5, 25, 25.5, 25.5)" [64.75, 64.75, 63. 5, 64.75, 64.75 cm] from cast on edge ending on a WS row, shape armhole:
Cast off 5 sts at beg of next 2 rows. Dec 1 st at both ends of next and ev foll alt row 2(4, 5, 7, 8) times in all, keeping patt correct – 66(68, 70, 72, 74)sts.

Back Neck Shaping
Cont until work measures 31(31, 31, 32, 32)" [78.75(78.75, 78.75, 81.25, 81.25)cm] from cast on edge, ending on WS row, work back neck:
Next row (RS)   Work 19(20, 19, 20, 21)sts, cast off centre 28(28, 32, 32, 32) sts, work to end. Join a second ball of yarn and work both sides at the same time, dec 1 st at both neck edges on next ev foll row 8 times – 11(12, 11, 12, 13) sts.
Cont until work measures 32.25(32.25, 32.25, 33.25, 33.25)" [82(82, 82, 84.5, 84.5)cm] from cast on edge ending on WS row, then
work shoulders:
Work and place 6 sts on holder at armhole edge on next row, (for left back neck it will be foll row), and 5(6,

5, 6, 7) sts on foll alternate row. Cast off over all 11(12, 11, 12, 13) sts.
Front Neck Shaping
At the same time as armhole shaping, when work measures 25.5(25.5, 25.5, 26, 26)" [64.75(64.75, 64.75, 66, 66)cm] from cast on edge ending on WS row, commence front neck:
Next row (RS)   Work 25(28, 23, 26, 27)sts, cast off centre 30(30, 32, 32, 34) sts, work to end. Join a second ball of yarn and work both sides at the same time, dec as foll:
1 st at both neck edges on next, then ev foll 3rd row 0(0, 3, 1, 0) times, then ev foll 4th row 5(5, 4, 6, 3) times, then ev foll 5th row 1(1, 0, 0, 3) times – 11(12, 11, 12, 13) sts.
Cont until work measures 32.25(32.25, 32.25, 33.25, 33.25)" [82(82, 82, 84.5, 84.5)cm] from cast on edge ending on WS row, then work shoulders:
Work and place 6 sts on holder at armhole edge on next row, (for left back neck it will be foll row), and 5(6, 5, 6, 7) sts on foll alternate row. Cast off over all 11(12, 11, 12, 13) sts.

SLEEVES
Using smaller needles, cast on 50(52, 56, 58, 60) sts. Work 4 rows in garter st, then change to larger nee-

dles and cont in st st to end inc as follows:
XS, S & M inc 1 st at both ends of 9th, then ev foll 10th row twice – 56(58, 62) sts
L   inc 1 st at both ends of 7th row 3 times, then ev 8th row once – 66 sts
XL   inc 1 st at both ends of 5th, then ev foll 6th row 4 times – 70 sts
Cont in patt as set until work measures 6" [15.25cm] from cast on edge ending on WS row and then shape sleeve cap:
Cast off 5 sts at beg of next 2 rows. Then dec 1 st at both ends of ev 3rd row 8(6, 8, 6, 2) times, then ev alt row 4(7, 6, 9, 15) times – 22(22, 24, 26, 26)sts.
Cast off 2 sts at beg of next 4 rows,. Cast off rem 14(14, 16, 18, 18) sts

FINISHING
Use a small neat backstitch on edge of work for all seams except welts, where an invisible slip stitch should be used. Join right shoulder seam.

Neckline edging
With right side facing, using smaller needles and starting at left shoulder, pick up and k18(18, 18, 20, 20) sts down straight front neck, k20(20, 20, 22, 22) sts down sloping neck edge, k28(28, 30, 30, 32) sts across centre

BOO CONT.

front, k20(20, 20, 22, 22) sts up sloping right front edge, k18(18, 18, 20, 20) sts up straight side of right neck edge, k10 sts down right back neck, k24(24, 28, 28, 28) sts across centre back and 10 sts up left neck edge – 148(148, 154, 162, 164) sts. Knit 3 rows and then cast off using

Picot point cast off

Cast off 2 sts, *slip rem st on RH needle onto LH needle, cast on 2 sts, cast off 4 sts; repeat from * to end and fasten off rem st.
Join left shoulder seam. Insert sleeves placing any fullness evenly over top of sleeve cap.

Sleeve edging

With right side facing, using smaller needles, pick up and k50(52, 56, 58, 60) sts. knit 1 row, then cast off using picot point cast-off as above. Join side and sleeve seams in one line.
Thread two or three (according to preference) lengths of ribbon through eyelets below bust and either join each one on inside at side seam or tie at centre front or back on outside.

STORM

SIZES

XS (to fit bust 32"/81cm)
S (to fit bust 34"/86cm)
M (to fit bust 36"/91cm)
L (to fit bust 38"/96cm)
XL (to fit bust 40"/101cm)
- see schematic for actual measurements.
Figures in parenthesis relate to S, M, L and XL sizes respectively. When there is only one figure, this relates to all.

YARN

ARTESANO Hummingbird: (327yds/300m per 150g hank):3(4, 4, 4, 4) hanks PEREGRINE

NEEDLES

3.5 mm (US 4) and 4 mm (US 6);
1 x 6.5mm (US 10.5) or size to obtain tension. We recommend Brittany Needles

TENSION

22 sts and 28 rows = 4"/10 cms over st st. Please work swatch and check carefully. If wrong alter size of needles until correct tension is achieved.

STITCHES

Garter Stitch
Knit every row
Stocking St   Knit every RS row and purl every WS row
Stamen Stitch Multiple of 2
Rows 1 & 3(RS)Using 6.5mm needle, knit
Row 2   Using 3.5mm needle, *k1, slip 1 purlwise; rep to last 2 sts, k2
Row 4   Using 3.5mm needle, k2, *slip 1 purlwise, k1; rep from * to end
Repeat these 4 rows

BACK

Using smaller needles, cast on 98(104,110, 116, 122) sts.
Work 8 rows in garter st and then change to larger needles and cont in st st to end, dec 1st at both ends of 19th, then ev 20th row 4 times in all – 90(96, 102, 108, 114) sts. Cont until work measures 13" [33 cm] from cast on edge, ending on WS row, then **shape armhole:**
Cast off 5(5, 5, 6, 6) sts at beg of next 2 rows. Dec 1 st at both ends of next and ev foll alt row 0(6, 9, 8, 14) times, then ev foll 3rd row 15(12, 11, 13, 9) times then ev foll 4th row 1(0, 0, 0, 0) times – 48(50, 52, 54, 56) sts.
Cast off.

LEFT FRONT
Using smaller needles, cast on 67(70, 73, 76, 79) sts. Work 8 rows in garter st as foll:

Row 1   knit
Row 2   p12, knit to end

Repeat these 2 rows 4 times, then change to larger needles and cont in st st to end as foll:

Next row   Work to last 13sts, p1, k to end

Next row   purl

These two rows form the st st patt, with purl st to mark foldline for band.

At the same time dec 1 st at beg of 19th then ev 20th row 4 times in all – 63(66, 69, 72, 75) sts.

Cont until work measures 13" [33 cm] from cast on edge, ending on WS row, **then shape armhole:**

Cast off 5(5, 5, 6, 6) sts at beg of next row. Work 1 row.

Dec 1 st at beg of next and ev foll alt row 0(6, 9, 8, 14) times, then at armhole edge on ev foll 3rd row 14(10, 9, 11, 7) times.

At the same time when there are 48(49, 50, 51, 52) sts, ending on RS row (11 rows from end of raglan decs), work neck shaping at same time, keeping raglan shaping correct:

Next row   Cast off 33(34, 35, 36, 37) sts, dec 1 st, work to end

Cont with raglan shaping

as above, working neckline shaping at same time by dec 1 st at neck edge on every row 11 times.

RIGHT FRONT
Work as for left front reversing all shapings and centre front band. Insert buttonholes when work measures 12.5 (12.5, 13, 13.5, 13.5)" [31.75(31.75, 33, 34.25, 34.25 cm] and 15.5(15.5, 16, 16.5, 16.5)" [39.25(39.25, 40.5, 42, 42) cm] ending on a WS row as foll:

K3, cast off 6 sts, k3, p1, k3, cast off 6 sts, work to end
Cast on the two sets of 6 sts when you come to them on next row, working into the backs of these sts on foll row.

SLEEVES
Using smaller needles, cast on 74(74, 80, 86, 90) sts and work 4 rows in garter st.. Then using two different size needles, work 5.25(5.25, 5.25, 5.75, 5.75)" [13.25(13.25, 13.25, 14.5, 14.5) cm] in Stamen St ending on row 2 or row 4. Work a further 4 rows in garter stitch on smaller needles, then change to larger needles and cont in st st to end, working first row as foll:
Next row (RS):
XS   k4, *k2tog, k3; rep from * to last 5 sts, k2tog, k3 - 60 sts

S   k4, *k2tog, k5; rep from * end - 64 sts
M   k6, *k2tog, k4; rep from * to last 2 sts, k2 - 68 sts
L   k2, *k2tog, k5; rep from * end - 74 sts
XL   k6, *k2tog, k5; rep from * to end - 78 sts
Cont until work measures 12(12, 12.5, 12.5, 12.5)" [30.5(30.5, 31.75, 31.75, 31.75)cm] from cast on edge ending on WS row and then **shape sleeve cap:**
Cast off 5(5, 5, 6, 6) sts at beg of next 2 rows. Then dec 1 st at both ends of next and then ev foll row 0(3, 7, 7, 11) times (48, 46, 42, 46, 42) sts, then ev alt row 17(16, 14, 16 14) times.
At the same time when there are 22 sts ending on WS row (for left sleeve it will be a RS row), **shape top of sleeve:**
Cast off 4 sts at beg of next and foll alt row, whilst cont with shaping on other side.
Cast off 5 sts at beg of next and foll alt row, whilst cont with shaping on other side.

FINISHING
Use a small neat backstitch on edge of work for all seams except cuffs, where an invisible slip stitch should be used. Turn back bands along purl st and slip stitch into place on inside along centre fronts and bottom edges. Sew two layers of

buttonholes together. Insert sleeves, joining the higher top sleeve edge to top back neck edge and lower top sleeve edge to top of fronts. Join side and sleeve seams in one line.

Collar

Using smaller needles, with RS facing, starting at right centre front edge, pick up and 21(22, 23, 24, 25) sts along horizontal neck edge, 24 sts up sloping neck edge and along top of right sleeve, 48(50, 52, 54, 56) sts across centre back, 24 sts along top of left sleeve and down sloping left neck edge and 21(22, 23, 24, 25) sts along horizontal left front neck edge – 138(142, 146, 150, 154) sts. Knit 1 row, then using two different size needles, work 2.25" [5.75 cm] in Stamen St, end on row 2 or row 4.

At the same time when 1" [2.5 cm] has been worked ending on WS row, work buttonhole:

Next row   Work 3 sts, cast off 6 sts, work to end. Cast on these sts when you come to them on next row, working into the backs of these sts on foll row.

Change to smaller needles and work 2 rows in garter stitch, then work a further 2.5" [6.25 cm] in st st, inserting buttonhole as above on the centre rows. Cast off loosely on larger needle if necessary. Turn collar back onto inside and slip stitch in place around neck edge. Neatly join side edges of collar at centre front and sew two layers of buttonhole together. Attach three buttons to left front band to correspond with buttonholes.

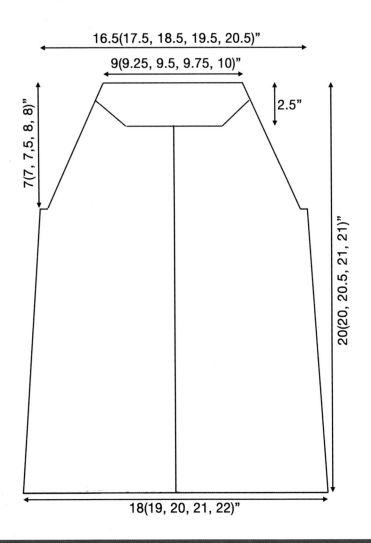

16.5(17.5, 18.5, 19.5, 20.5)"

9(9.25, 9.5, 9.75, 10)"

2.5"

7(7, 7.5, 8, 8)"

20(20, 20.5, 21, 21)"

18(19, 20, 21, 22)"

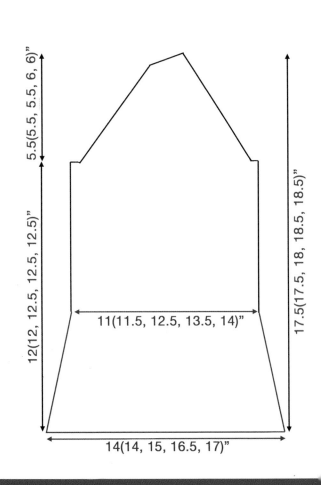

5.5(5.5, 5.5, 6, 6)"

12(12, 12.5, 12.5, 12.5)"

11(11.5, 12.5, 13.5, 14)"

17.5(17.5, 18, 18.5, 18.5)"

14(14, 15, 16.5, 17)"